Needlecraft Projects

Needlecraft Projects

PATRICIA RILEY

B T Batsford Limited
London

First published 1978
ISBN 0 7134 0745 X

Printed and bound in Great Britain by
Cox and Wyman Ltd, Fakenham
for the publishers
B T Batsford Limited
4 Fitzhardinge Street
London W1H 0AH

Contents

Introduction

This book is intended to help students of needlework, particularly those who are required to produce projects or studies to support their examination work.

The first five sections are in the form of basic instruction in various aspects of needlecraft and are complete in themselves. It is hoped that they will serve as an introduction to these topics and encourage interest in them. The final section aims to give clear and comprehensive guidance on the preparation of individual projects.

1 Appliqué

1 Appliqué

This dressed print is a form of appliqué popular in the early part of this century

A fourteenth-century knight wearing a surcoat decorated with heraldic emblems

Appliqué is a form of embroidery which can be done quite quickly and which can be used to create rich and dramatic effects. Basically appliqué is the technique of cutting out shapes in material and applying them by a variety of stitching methods to a separate piece of material.

Early examples

Appliqué work was done by the early Egyptians, Greeks and Romans. In the exotic embroideries of India mirror fragments, called Shisha glass, are used, applied to the background fabric with chain stitches. In Britain in Norman times men wore tunics which had a fitted bodice widening to a full skirt which was often decorated with bands of appliqué work round the neck, hem, wrists and sometimes the upper arm.

For hundreds of years appliqué embroidery has been used in church work, for banners, wall hangings and, in fact, everywhere a boldly decorative effect would be appreciated.

Fabrics and thread

Materials of different kinds can be used in one piece of work, although it is much easier to work with firmly woven fabrics, such as cotton, as the pieces have a clean edge when they are cut. Materials which are very fine or stretchy are best avoided by a beginner but if it is necessary to use them for a particular effect then they can be backed with iron-on interfacing which makes them more manageable. It is important that the background fabric should be stronger than the materials which are to be sewn on. If a lighter weight fabric is chosen for the background then it must be mounted on a firm material, such as unbleached calico, before beginning to sew.

Materials are best stored in clear plastic bags. If these are kept according to colour it helps the job of finding the right piece. A special bag can be kept in which to keep very small scraps, bits of felt, broken jewellery, sequins, feathers.

As far as threads are concerned it is good to have a wide selection from which to choose. In most cases any embroidery stitches are used to define and accent the design as the pieces themselves are the main decorative element. Quite often threads are couched on to the fabric for decoration or to disguise edges.

Couching

A wide variety of threads may be couched, ranging from metal threads, wool, cord or even string.

Using a frame

Most appliqué work can be done in the hand but the use of a frame helps to prevent puckering of the applied pieces and would help to ensure a more accurate reproduction of the design.

Basically there are three main types of frame.
1 The circular frame which can be held in the hand or used with a clamp or stand.

The round or hoop frame usually has a screw to adjust the size of the outer ring

2   The rectangular frame with screw adjustments.
3   The rectangular frame which is adjusted by pegs which slot into holes in the side pieces of the frame.

When using a frame for appliqué it is best to keep the frame quite slack until all the pieces are tacked on with a small stitch about 1 cm from the edge. The frame should then be tightened and the outline worked in the chosen way.

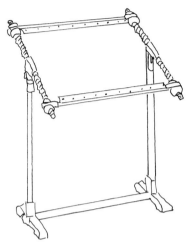

The side bars of this rectang-ular frame are made with screw ends for tightening the work. It can be used without the floor stand as this is detachable

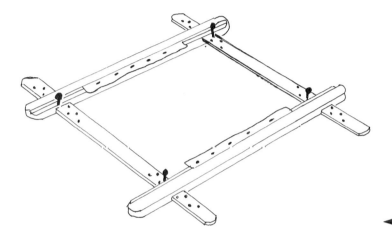

◄   *Square adjustable frame*

Methods of working a design

There are two major decisions to be made when doing a piece of appliqué embroidery. The first and perhaps the most difficult is the question of design and the second is technical. The technical question concerns the methods to be used to attach the pieces to get the best effect. It is best to become familiar with all the different methods by doing a sampler or samplers. Possibly more than one method will be used in a picture, for example where a wide variety of fabrics may be chosen.

Easy appliqué

Appliqué is easy when the materials chosen do not fray. These could be leather, felt or any other fabric which has been coated with an adhesive or backed with iron-on interfacing. This is because the pieces can be cut to the finished shape right away and can be arranged or re-arranged until a satisfactory effect is achieved. The edges can be sewn down using a simple running stitch, an embroidery stitch or a hemming stitch. The edges can then be neatened or emphasized with couching or braid. The main point is that the neatening of the edges is purely a matter of choice and not one of necessity.

*Simple appliqué using felt held
down with small running stitches*

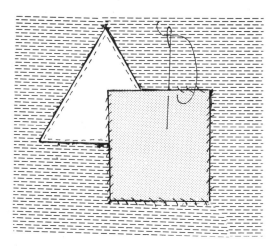

Simple appliqué

Machined appliqué
If the sewing machine is a straight stitch machine, then materials
to be applied which fray will have to be mounted on iron-on

interfacing or have the edges turned in before they can be machined close to the edges.

Where a swing needle machine is available the pieces can be cut to the finished size right away and then be machined in place, using a decorative machine stitch or the standard zigzag stitch. If the material is stretchy or very light-weight it is better to cut the pieces 1 cm larger, machine along the actual design line and trim the surplus material away close to the machining.

The seam allowance must be clipped before it is turned over the interfacing

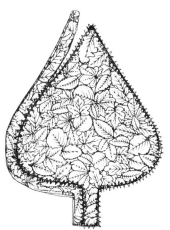

Machined appliqué

Machined appliqué using a variety of stitches

Blind stitched appliqué

This method is widely used. It is quick to do and is used where the pieces which are to be attached are made of fraying materials. Basically the method consists of cutting the pieces large enough to allow a turning to be made.

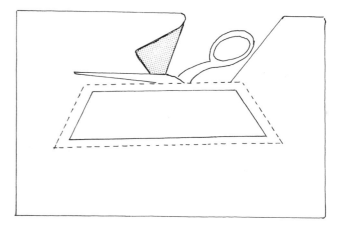

The amount of turning will vary according to the weight of the material and how much it frays. A difficult fabric, such as silk, could be handled more easily if a piece of iron-on interfacing, cut to the finished shape could be put on the silk before it is cut out. For a fabric such as a medium weight cotton a good seam allowance would be 0.5 cm. The piece can then be

A sampler showing a method of working blind stitched appliqué

Blind stitched appliqué. The Clown's trousers have been caught down to give a quilted effect. His hands and feet are made of leather   *Heather Lewis*

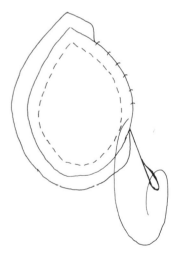

The seam allowance can be 'stroked' under with the needle as the piece is hemmed in place

tacked on to the background 1 cm from the raw edge. It is quite easy to work round the piece with a hemming stitch, stroking the seam allowance to the inside with the point of the needle as the work proceeds.

The tacking line acts as a guide as to how far to push the raw edge inside which means that it is not necessary to draw the outline in any way on to the piece.

Where larger pieces or simple shaped pieces are being applied it might be found easier to turn the allowance in and tack it down before applying the piece to the background.

Embroidered appliqué carried out entirely in buttonhole stitch by Gillian Matkin

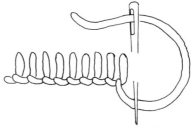

Buttonhole stitch

Embroidered appliqué

Pieces of fabric can be attached to the background using embroidery stitches. The most commonly used stitches are buttonhole, chain and satin.

Usually the pieces are cut a little larger than the finished shape. The design edge is embroidered and the excess trimmed carefully up to the embroidery stitches. If the pieces are firm and easy to handle they can be cut to the finished size, hemmed down lightly and then embroidered.

Chain stitch

◄ *Satin stitch*

Appliqué panel which makes use of a great many different methods of sewing on the pieces of fabric

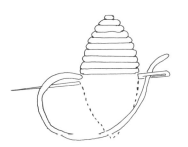

*Several pieces might be tried
before the right one is found*

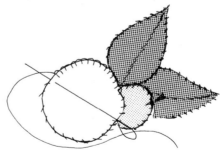

Embroidered appliqué

Inlaid appliqué

Instead of sewing the shapes on to the background pieces, the contrasting fabrics which make up the design can be attached from the back. The outline of the shape is embroidered or machine-stitched through the background material and the attached piece. The shape is then cut out of the background fabric to reveal the material underneath. The inlay work technique has been particularly developed by the Indian women in

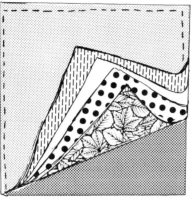

Several layers of different material are tacked together

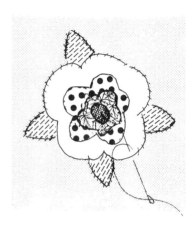

the Sans Blas Islands. They may use as many as five or six layers of fabric in different colours which are tacked together round the edges.

Parts are then cut away to reveal the different colours. The raw edges are turned in and slip stitched into place. They call this Mola work or cut work.

Inlaid appliqué

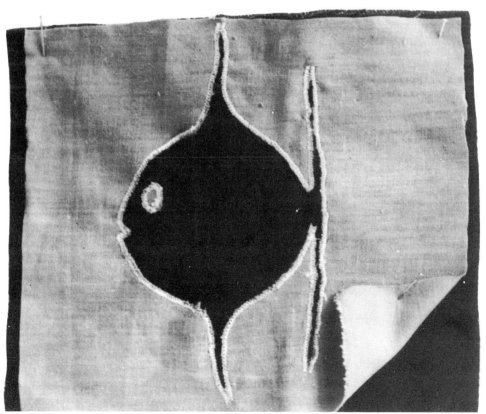

Appliqué on net

This type of applique is often found on curtains, bedspreads, mats and dresses. As in appliqué generally, bold clear designs are best. The design should be traced on to firm white calico or stiff paper. The net should be tacked to this with a piece of lawn on top. The design, which can be seen through the net and the lawn should be outlined with an embroidery stitch.

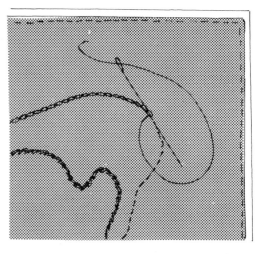

Two semi-transparent fabrics tacked together with the design outlined in chain stitch and stem stitch

The lawn or the net are cut away according to the design.

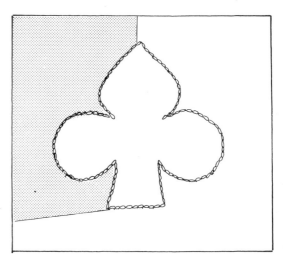

Another way of using these fabrics is to trace the design on to the lawn. The net is tacked to this and the design outlined with running stitches and then embroidered before the surplus fabric is trimmed away.

Designing for appliqué

There are several ways in which the question of design may be tackled.

1 Free appliqué. Pieces of material can be cut up, arranged on the backgound and sewn on.

2 Paper shapes. Pieces of paper may be cut out free hand and arranged on a background to form the basis of a design or the paper could be folded and cut to make a symmetrical design.

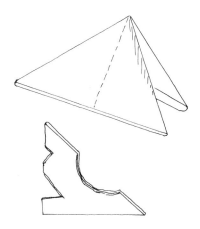

Fold a piece of paper and cut pieces out of the sides

◄ *The paper opened out then has a symmetrical design*

3 Shapes may be drawn round such as leaves, keys, egg cups, geometrical shapes such as triangles, squares or circles.

4 A picture perhaps from a Christmas card or a children's story book, could be adapted.

Simple shapes make effective appliqué

It is useful to have a folder in which to keep pictures, drawings or illustrations which might prove a source of inspiration.

*The size and shape of the
background should relate to
the design*

Appliqué is a bold type of embroidery and small details are best filled in with embroidery stitches or left out. The design should have good over all proportions. The size and shape of the background matters. A tall and narrow background might look most attractive for a single flower. Shapes should be related to each other and not scattered in an isolated fashion. The horizon should divide the picture into thirds rather than into two halves. A sense of distance can be achieved through the use of colour, tone and size.

Before settling on the final design the pieces should be pinned on to the background and the work held away pinned on a wall or if this is impossible, stand on a chair and look down on the work from as great a distance as possible. Often any glaring errors in balance can be spotted if the work is looked at through a mirror.

The background fabric often sets the tone for the work. Hessian, denim, drill, calico, striped and pattered fabrics can be used. In some cases the original design may be merely enhanced rather than re-processed or re-created. Old clothes can be used with an eye open for worn parts. The dullest backgrounds are a good foil for bright and vivid colours. Black sets off applied pieces most effectively.

Transferring the design

The design can be traced on to the background fabric using dressmakers' carbon paper. The drawing itself can then be cut up and the shapes used as patterns to cut out the pieces to be applied. If squared paper is used for the drawing, then when the pieces are cut out it is easy to make sure that the grain of the pieces matches the grain of the background fabric. This helps to ensure that the work is not puckered.

If marks on the materials are kept to the minimum the design can be adapted as the work is in progress. It is possible to omit marking the background fabric and, by using an extra copy of the original drawing as a guide, arrange the pieces of fabric to be applied straight on to the background.

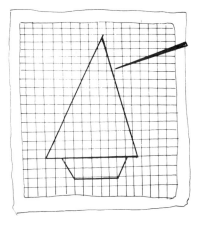

The design is traced from the squared paper on to the background fabric

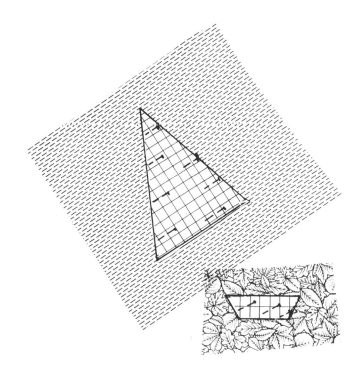

The squared paper is cut up and the pieces used as patterns. The grain of the material must match the squares

Appliqué as a project

1 Make a collection of pieces of material and store these in plastic bags according to colour. Larger pieces which might be useful for backgrounds can be kept folded separately.

2 Keep a sketch book and collect in a scrap book or envelope folder pictures which are attractive and which might adapt for use as appliqué designs, bearing in mind that boldness is a characteristic of this work. There could be tracings from children's books, greetings cards, experiments with cut paper, arrangements of geometrical shapes, simple shapes from nature or household objects.

3 Make a series of samplers to try out the various methods of attaching materials together. These can be mounted on card and included in the project folder.

4 Try working the same design with different background colours and different colours for the pieces to see the effect colour has on the completed work.

5 Find out from books, museums, cathedrals, what uses have been made of applique in the past. Try to see examples of such appliqué work. These can be photographed or sketched and described.

6 Where is appliqué used today? Examples can be sketched or photographed.

7 Plan a piece of work which will be a worthwhile illustration of this kind of embroidery. This could be a picture or wall panel, a bedspread, a tablecloth, a mat or even an article of clothing.

2 Cross stitch

2 Cross stitch

Background to this embroidery

Cross stitch is included among the oldest stitches which have been used. It is found in English Medieval embroidery along with stem stitch, tent stitch, split stitch and underside couching.

It is easy embroidery to work, as generally only one stitch is used throughout. It may have originated in Russia, Norway, Germany or Italy, or possibly in all of them. Examples of this work from European and Middle Eastern countries are interesting to study as the colours and designs are often typical

Cross stitch used to make a picture. A typical piece of mid-nineteenth century embroidery

Late nineteenth century garland embroidered with pastel colours

of certain regions. Persian cross-stitch for instance shows a marked preference for the use of plant forms and blue, red and green are often used together in one design. The effect is usually rich and dramatic. The beauty of this kind of embroidery depends on design, regularity of the stitches and the choice of colours and these are often bright. It has been popular in peasant societies and represents the embroidery of working people.

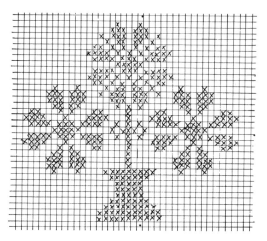

It is suitable for decorating household articles such as curtains, towels, mats, bedspreads as well as dresses, blouses, pinafores, overalls.

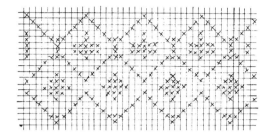

◄ *Regular geometric patterns are very easy to work out*

Evenly woven material has the same number of threads to the 25 mm measured either along the warp or the weft

How a cross stitch design is worked

The method of working depends on the kind of material chosen. On smooth materials any of the usual methods of marking a design on to fabric can be used. A pattern or picture could be transferred using dressmakers' carbon paper and the cross stitches worked over the crosses marked on the material. Transfers too can be bought and ironed on to any smooth fabric.

The most popular method is to work on a fairly coarse evenly woven material where the warp and weft threads which make up the fabric can easily be counted.

The design is drawn on squared paper. This is copied on to the fabric by counting the squares then counting the threads on the fabric. It is usual to begin by tacking a line through the centre of the fabric and drawing a line down the middle of the design. This ensures that the design is placed accurately on the fabric. Two lines are often needed, horizontal and vertical.

Where the material will not accept a transfer and the fabric is not evenly woven the design can be worked over a piece of canvas tacked on to the background fabric. The stitches are worked over the threads of the canvas, through the material underneath and when it is finished the canvas threads are drawn out. The stitches must be kept fairly tight as they will be looser when the canvas threads are removed.

—— weft ◄————

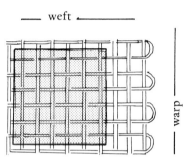

| warp |

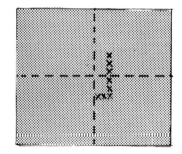

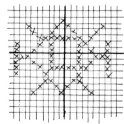

Lines of tacking are used to position the design correctly

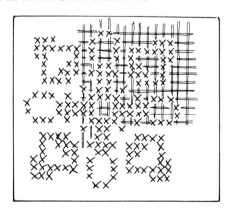

◄ *The canvas threads are drawn out after the design has been worked*

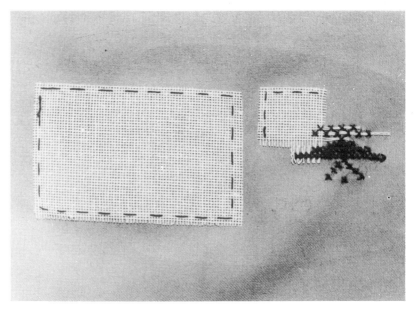

Cross stitch over canvas on a finely woven cotton fabric. The threads of the canvas are easily drawn

Fabric and thread

Almost any kind of material can be used for cross stitch. For fine materials, silks, lawns, muslins it is best to mark the design on to the fabric. The canvas method works on velvet, rough serges, denim. For the counting method canvas, scrim, Hardanger cloth, fairly coarse linen, or any other fabric which is evenly woven will be satisfactory.

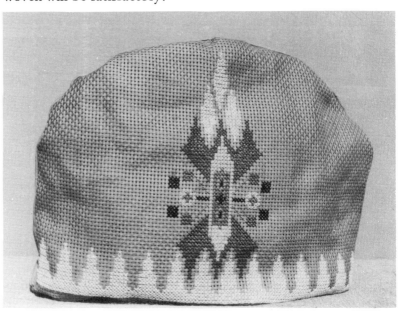

Cross stitch on binca by Fiona McCulloch

For work on open backgrounds wool needles with blunt points and long eyes are best.

The working threads may be silk, wool, cotton or linen but the weight of the thread must be suited to the fabric on which it is to be used. Too fine a thread will look spidery, while too heavy a thread will look clumsy. A rough guide is to compare the thickness of the threads used to make up the background with the embroidery threads. Too wide a difference in thickness will not usually produce an attractive effect. The threads should be pulled through the fabric fairly firmly otherwise the finished effect may be rather untidy.

How to cross stitch
Do not begin with a knot. Either start with an oblique half-cross stitch under the first cross stitch or hold the end of the thread at the back of the work and make sure that it is caught and held by the stitches on the back of the material as the design is worked on the front.

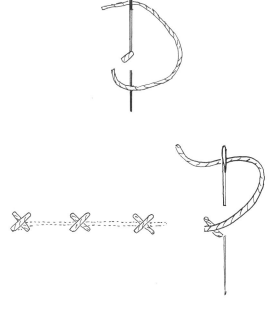

Begin with a small stitch under the first half of the cross The new thread can be held at the back of the work and caught down with the back of the stitches

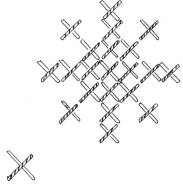

Every stitch should take up the same number of threads each way. This may be in the region of between one and four. Unless a semi-transparent material is being used where threads carried across the back would show, each stitch must be crossed the same way to keep the work looking neat.

The stitches must all be crossed the same way. A stitch in the corner of the work is a useful reminder

Stitches are worked according to which method is most convenient for the embroiderer.

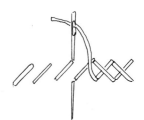

Each cross may be completed as the design is worked

A whole row of under stitches can be worked and then a row of stitches can be done to finish off the stitch

The back of the stitches might look like this or this

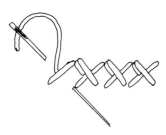

What is thought to be the original and earliest Italian method of working cross stitch resulted in a double sided cross stitch. If each cross is to be finished before the next one is started an extra stitch is needed on the right side from the centre hole upwards to the left, to bring the thread into the correct position for making the second stitch on the wrong side.

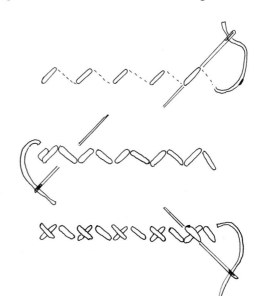

Double sided cross stitch gives a similar effect on either side of the work

Double sided cross stitch can be worked more easily in rows. The half stitch is needed to correct the stitch at the beginning of the row

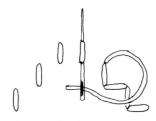

Holbein or double running stitch

Variations on cross stitch

There are many variations in the way that a cross stitch can be worked, although these are mainly used in canvas work. Occasionally Holbein or double running stitch is used to emphasize parts of the design.

Double cross stitch must be worked over two or four threads of the background fabric. A straight cross is sewn over the oblique one.

A sampler using cross stitch with oblong cross stitch in the colours of the forest scene

Double cross stitch

Two-sided Italian cross stitch

This version of two-sided Italian cross stitch and long armed cross stitch are also used.

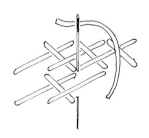

Long-armed cross stitch

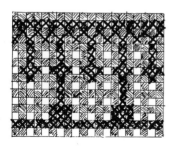

Cross stitch on gingham

Assissi work

Cross stitch on gingham

Gingham is a cotton fabric with bands of alternately coloured threads running the length of the warp and crossing the width or weft in the same order. This makes a checked pattern which has alternate squares of strong colour, white and a shade half way between the two. The squares vary in size from less than 0.5 cm to more than 4 cm. For a cross stitch design up to 0.5 cm square is easy to handle. If a larger check is used the cross stitches need to be held down with another small cross stitch in the centre of the large one.

A wide variety of effects can be created not only by using different coloured embroidery threads, but by working the design on the light squares or on the dark. This particular kind of cross stitch is effective when used for blouses, children's clothes and table linen.

Assisi work

In this version of cross stitch the stitches instead of forming the design itself are used as a background completely filling in all the space not occupied by it.

Assisi is a small Italian village which is famous because of its association with St Francis. It has also given its name to this particular kind of embroidery. Many fine examples of this work contain motifs and characters taken from the life of the saint. Very often the embroidery is in red and or blue stitches on pale ivory linen.

Assisi embroidery is worked in three stages:
1 The design is outlined with a row of running stitches.
2 A second row of running stitches is worked back, filling in the spaces so a continuous line is formed.
This is the Holbein or double running stitch part of the design.
3 The background round the pattern is filled in with cross stitch, half of each stitch being made first and then the crossing stitches being worked on top.

Designing for cross stitch

Many embroidery designs can be adapted for cross stitch. The design can be traced through a sheet of carbon paper on to graph paper. If the graph paper is then coloured with crayons or felt tip pens, squaring the edges of the shapes at the same time, then the graph paper can be used as a chart from which to work.

Almost any object can be adapted for cross stitch.

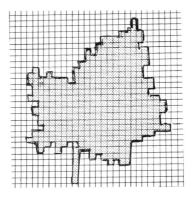

A leaf shape adapted for working in cross stitch. The original leaf drawing was copied on to squared paper with carbon paper and then it was 'squared' off

Many objects have a symbolical meaning, for example a ship is a symbol of hope.

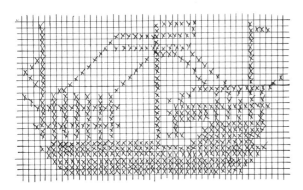

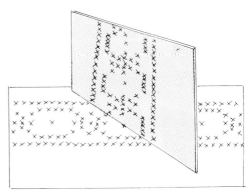

A mirror is useful for adapting a straight edge border for a corner

To adapt a straight border design so that it will work out round a corner a mirror can be used. The mirror should be held on its side on a suitable part of the design so that an exact reproduction of the design can be seen going in a direction at right angles to the original line.

This variation on the design will then have to be copied on to graph paper.

Cross stitch samplers

This is probably the most well known application of cross stitch work. The earliest samplers were made in the sixteenth century although apparently there are none of these still in existence. There are some seventeenth century samplers and these show the order in which a child learned different stitches. They have the name of the person who made them and the date when they were completed. They are covered with scattered motifs, birds and geometric patterns on loosely woven linen fabric. These appear to have been test pieces.

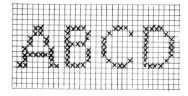

Letters adapted for cross stitch

The sampler would be added to when a new skill had to be mastered. A wide variety of stitches and patterns would be incorporated.

These early samplers became a more carefully considered article generally made by girls between the ages of seven and eleven. By the eighteenth century the sampler had developed into an item to be framed and used for decoration. Cross stitch was usually the only stitch used and the work often included the alphabet, a text or poem and a border. There was often a house, trees, people and objects which were associated with the personal life of the embroiderer. There are many examples of Victorian samplers worked in cross stitch on fine woollen canvas still to be seen in museums, stately homes and private houses too.

Cross stitch as a project

1   Look at as many books as you can on cross stitch. Look too at books on embroidery which may have a section on cross stitch.
2   Study as many cross stitch designs as possible. Keep a record either by photographs or sketches or even a chart on which the following information could be recorded:

Country of origin	Article	Description of design	Background fabric	Thread	Colours	Stitches

3   Draw diagrams to show how cross stitches are formed and then try them on pieces of material.
4   Work some cross stitch patterns on a variety of materials, using different threads.
5   Work several patterns in various combinations of colours to study the different effects.
6   Make a sample to show Assisi embroidery.
7   Try out the technique of using canvas over the background and drawing out the threads of the canvas after the cross stitches have been worked.
8   Try some cross stitch on gingham and look at the varied effects caused by working on just the dark squares or just the light.
9   Work out some geometrical designs on squared paper.
10   Practise 'squaring off' drawings of objects such as birds, using tracing paper, graph paper and crayons.
11   Decide on a finished article which will show an understanding of the skill of cross stitch. This might be a sampler or perhaps even a Christmas table cloth using a red even-weave fabric and white thread.

3 Canvas work

3 Canvas work

A definition

Canvas work is the name given to a form of embroidery which is done on canvas or coarse linen. The whole of the background fabric is covered with stitches. When the entire design is worked in petit point or gros point the finished effect looks like woven tapestry and so it is often called needlework-tapestry.

There are a great many canvas work stitches and these are worked over a single thread or several threads of the background fabric.

The aspects of canvas work which are particularly appealing are the variety of effects which can be achieved not only with colour but also with texture. Today the accent is on individual design and once the basic skills have been mastered, designs are not difficult to create.

Canvas work of the past

Canvas work was popular in England and Europe from the early sixteenth century until the mid eighteenth century. During this time book covers were made using tent stitch in silk on linen and wool and silk on canvas and linen were often used for the upholstery of chairs and table carpets. A table carpet which can be seen in the Victorian and Albert Museum and which is known as the Bradford Carpet has been worked in silk tent stitch with a fineness of about 400 stitches in a 25mm square. Other carpets which can be seen there have been worked with long-armed cross and cross-stitches too.

Canvas work today

Canvas work is particularly hard wearing when wool is used for the embroidery. Wall panels or pictures are popular made in canvas work but it is really particularly useful for cushions, chair seats and upholstery while the coarser canvas is used for rugmaking, using the traditional canvas work stitches. Smaller items such as belts, bags and boxes are also attractive made in canvas work.

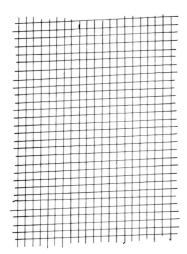

Single thread canvas

Double thread canvas ➤

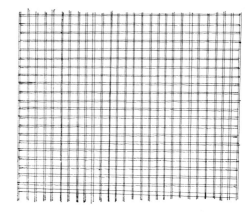

Fabric and thread

Although any evenly woven fabric could be used for canvas work it is unwise to waste time and money working on anything but the best quality background fabrics. It is important that the fabric is firm, supple and of course evenly woven.

There are two types of canvas:

Often single thread canvas is classified according to the number of threads there are to an inch.

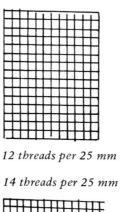
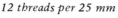

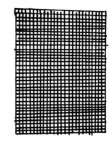

12 threads per 25 mm   *16 threads per 25 mm*   *24 threads per 25 mm*

14 threads per 25 mm   *18 threads per 25 mm*   *28 threads per 25 mm*

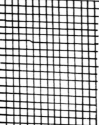

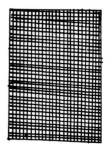

Single canvas

Double thread canvas is sometimes classified according to the number of holes to 25 mm.

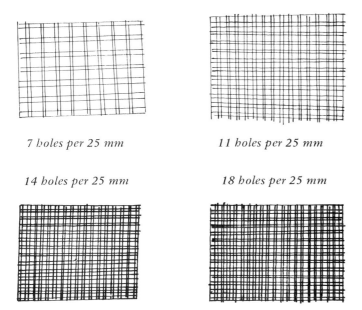

7 *holes per 25 mm*   11 *holes per 25 mm*

14 *holes per 25 mm*   18 *holes per 25 mm*

Double canvas

Canvas with between three and seven holes to 25mm (1 in.) is generally known as rug canvas.

The numbers of threads to 25mm can vary from **32** for very fine work to 4 but the most useful size is about 18 threads to 25mm which will take fine and coarser stitches giving a variety of effects.

Double thread canvas is not the best to start with because the range of stitches which can be worked is restricted. When it is used each thread should be counted regardless of the spacing.

The correct needles are sold as tapestry or rug needles in various sizes. They are without points so that they will slip easily through the holes in the canvas. The right needle is one which will thread fairly easily with an eye just large enough to carry the thread.

The thread most commonly used on canvas is Crewel wool, or Tapestry wool. The correct number of threads to use in the needle at one time is that which, when the chosen stitch is being worked, covers the threads of the canvas completely. Other yarns can be used ranging from silk, raffia, knitting wools, mettalic threads or carpet thrums.

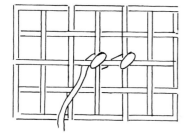

Tent stitch

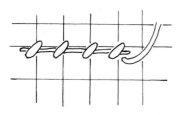

Tent stitch worked over a tramme thread

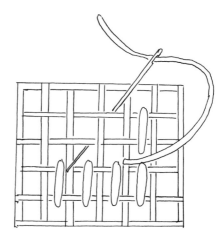

Upright Gobelin stitch

Stitches

Petit point or tent stitch

This is perhaps the most widely used stitch in canvas work and can be done in any direction, from right to lift, left to right or even up or down. Gros point is a larger edition of petit point.

Sometimes these stitches are used over a laid thread which is known as Trammé. These threads which lie between the stitches and the canvas give a slightly raised effect and increase the covering quality of the stitches. The same colour thread is used for the trammé and the stitch.

Upright gobelin stitch

This is a frequently used canvas work stitch. Occasionally whole designs are worked in upright gobelin although it is more commonly used for backgrounds. This stitch can be worked either from left to right or from right to left.

Gobelin stitch

This is worked in the same way as tent stitch but the stitches slant over one thread in width and two in height.

Half cross stitch

This gives the same effect at the front as tent stitch but short upright stitches are formed on the back. This is more economical on thread but does not have the same covering quality as tent stitch and so it is frequently trammed.

Cross stitch

It is necessary when working cross stitch to ensure that all the crosses have the top stitch slanting in the same direction and this is usually from left to right. There are many variations on the basic cross stitch.

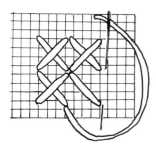 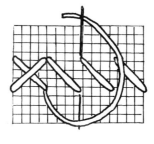

Cross stitch can be formed by working one stitch at a time or by doing them in groups

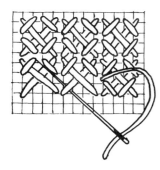

◄ *Rice stitch*

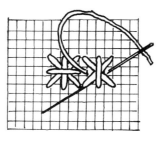

Double cross, Leviathan or Smyrna

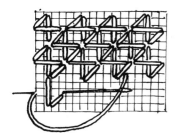

◄ *Diagonal cross — worked diagonally from bottom right to top left*

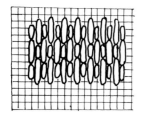

Hungarian (mosaic when worked diagonally)

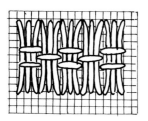

Upright Gobelin with cross bars darned

There is some dispute as to how many canvas work stitches there are, some experts putting the total in the region of 200. Many stitches are a variation of a development of the basic upright and slanting stitches although some are a little bit more complicated.

Brick stitch

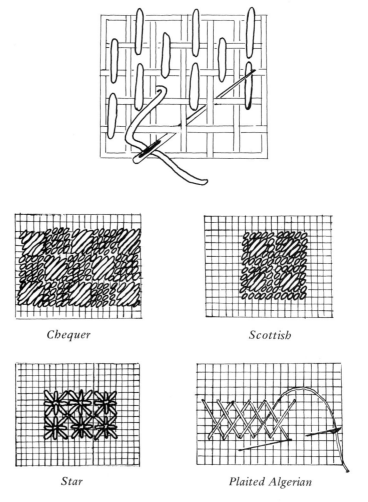

Chequer

Scottish

Star

Plaited Algerian

One interesting development of upright stitches has acquired a variety of names. Sometimes known as Florentine, Bargello, Hungarian work or Flame Embroidery this work makes use of perpendicular stitches which can be the same length or combinations of long and short, covering two to six meshes of the canvas.

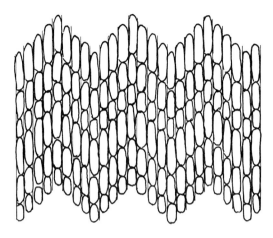

Florentine stitch

Traditionally several shades of one colour are used or some-times two or three main colours together with shades of these colours.

These stitches are sufficient for a wide range of work to be carried out.

A view from the window gives an opportunity to put together a wide variety of stitches

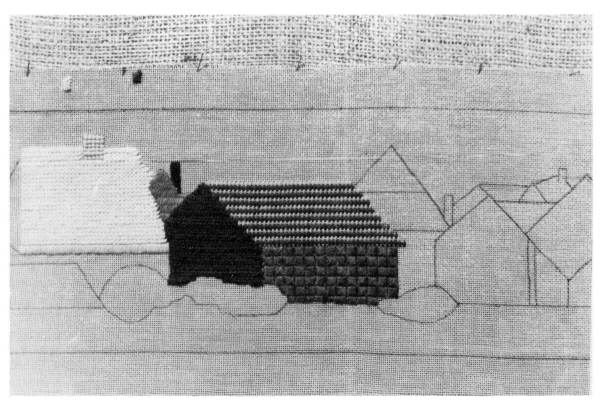

A stool top using only blues and greens. The effect is made much more interesting by the use of a variety of stitches in blue against a background of pale green tent stitch

Designs for canvas work embroidery

There are a great many decisions to make when beginning a piece of work and it can be difficult to decide where to begin. A small picture makes a good starting piece because a wide variety of stitches can be included.

Draw the picture on squared paper. Changes may well have already begun to take place as details are left out or made more important to fit in with the squares or to make a more satisfactory effect.

Find a picture which is attractive or interesting

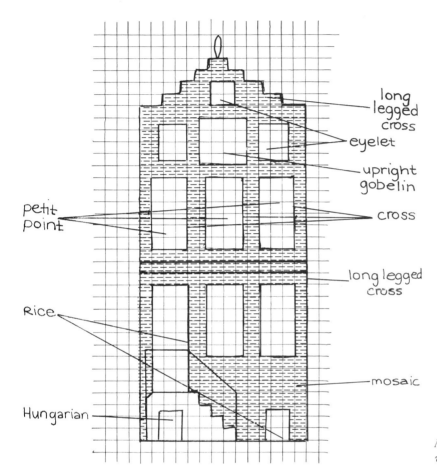

long legged cross

eyelet

upright gobelin

petit point

cross

long legged cross

Rice

mosaic

Hungarian

Make a note of the stitches which will be used

Re-draw the picture so that it corresponds with the finished size of the work. Crayon or paint it. Try the stitches out on a piece of spare canvas making sure that the right number of strands are being used in the needle. Cut a piece of canvas about 10 cm bigger all round than the finished design and oversew the edges so that they will not fray while working.

Start working at the top of the design following the squared chart. Do not use too much wool in the needle as it wears thin as it is pulled in and out of the canvas.

An alternative method is to draw the design on the canvas using waterproof ink. If the original drawing is placed behind the canvas the outlines can usually be seen and copied through.

Another way is to outline the design on the canvas with a running stitch which can be worked through a tracing of the design attached to the canvas which can be torn off before beginning to work the design.

A finished sampler

Commercial design

Canvas work designs can be bought already printed on canvas. In some cases the whole of the trammé grounding is done in the colours appropriate to the finished piece. This is pleasant and relaxing embroidery and could perhaps be a good way to develop a rhythm for working canvas stitches.

Finishing off canvas work

Canvas work is best worked in a rectangular frame as sometimes the stitches tend to pull the canvas out of shape while it is being worked. When work is done in the hand any mis-shaping which occurs can be corrected after the work is finished. When a piece of canvas work is finished it should be stretched before it is mounted into its finished position.

To stretch a piece of canvas work a board is needed which is larger than the embroidery. Drawing pins and a piece of blotting paper or sheeting are also needed.

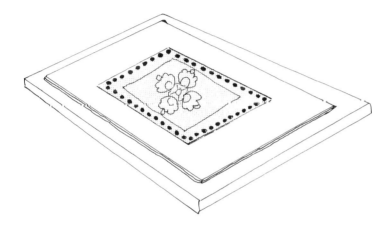

To stretch the work lay it face up on sheets of damp blotting paper. Pull it into shape before fastening it down with drawing pins

Pin the centre of each edge first and then put in additional pins at about 4-centimetre intervals until the work is lying quite flat and tight. This should be left overnight or until it has dried. Sometimes if the work has become badly out of shape it is necessary to stretch it more than once.

A canvas work project

1 Collect samples of the various canvases and fabrics which would make suitable backgrounds.
2 Make a collection of different threads and yarns.
3 Using single thread canvas with 18 holes to 25 mm make samples showing a variety of stitches. These could be worked individually and then in combinations.
4 Make a collection of pictures, illustrations, sketches which might adapt for canvas work.
5 Get some books on canvas work and begin to make notes on materials, stitches, preparation of work, finishing off and making up.
6 Find some books on design and read the suggestions on how to make up individual designs for canvas work. These

could include using cut paper, arrangement of geometrical shapes. Make notes on designing for canvas work.

7 Try out some abstract designs on paper. Work these up to a stage where they are ready to be worked on canvas, planning the stitches to be used and the colour schemes. Keep these for the project folder section on design.

8 Find out whether there are any examples of canvas work in museums or houses open to the public which it would be convenient to go and see. Sometimes it is possible to buy photographs of these or alternatively they could be photographed or drawn and described.

9 Plan a piece of finished work to incorporate a variety of stitches using a personal design.

4 Patchwork

4 Patchwork

Patchwork is the art of making designs by joining small pieces of odd materials together. Patience and the ability to work neatly are necessary to do successful patchwork. The attraction of this work is in the choice and arrangements of the shapes and materials.

Early examples of this work often had materials arranged in a hit-or-miss way but particularly from the middle of the eighteenth century the patterns have been copied from old Mosaics, Parquet designs and also from geometrical figures.

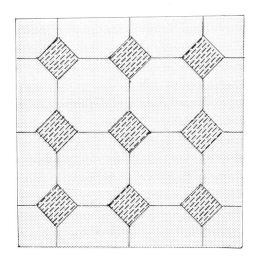

Dutch tile pattern

Today patchwork is made in the traditional way as well as in a more flexible style which has resulted in the deliberate attempts which have been made to explore new ways of using the craft.

Fabrics for patchwork
As a general rule fabrics should be of similar weight, weave and fibre content. For example, the material which is ideally suited to this work is cotton poplin and it would be a good idea to use something like this for a first piece. Keep in mind that linen, flannel, leather and many other materials can be used.

Cushions using hexagons and squares Left: Kim Taylor Right: Edwina Mountain

Satin and velvet together can produce a very attractive effect. When the basic skills have been mastered different effects can be experimented with. There are some fabrics which are best avoided for various reasons:

Materials which fray easily.

Heavy materials which cannot be tacked down easily over the paper patch.

Fabrics which stretch, such as jersey

Using washable and unwashable pieces in the same article.

Worn materials. Discarded clothes or curtains are very useful to the patchworker but care must be taken to pick out the unworn pieces.

Using old and new materials together without washing the new, just in case they shrink.

Colour and pattern

The choice of colours and patterns is of course a very personal thing. If a bit box is available go through it picking out pieces of cotton material which are similar in weight and are attractive.

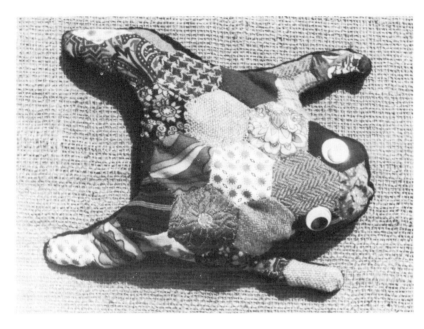

A toy frog made with hexagon shapes by Kim Taylor

If a particular article is to be made care must be taken that there is enough material to finish it. If there is no bit box a favourite dress or shirt which has been discarded might make a good starting point. It might be necessary to buy a small amount of material to go with this.

Patchwork based on a 'taking a line for a walk' pattern

Additional requirements before beginning

As well as fabric, stiff paper is needed to make the paper shapes which are tacked into the fabric to hold the patches firm. Magazines are ideal for this. Scissors are needed to cut the fabric patches and another pair to cut the paper. Needles should be as fine as can be comfortably worked with. Pins should be fine and made of steel to prevent leaving holes in the fabric. The thread should be matched with the fabric, silk for silk, cotton for cotton, man-made sewing thread with man-made fabrics.

Finally, unless crazy patchwork is being made, templates are necessary. Templates are basically of two kinds:

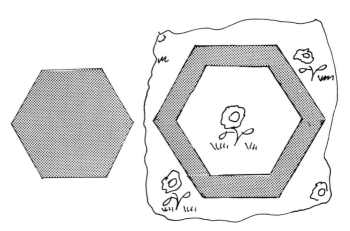

Solid template

Window template

The templates most commonly used are solid. These are the actual size of the finished patch. The window template is useful if a patterned material is being used and some particular part of the design is to be centred on the patch.

Templates are made from metal, perspex or very stiff card. These can be bought from needlecraft shops or made. If they are made it is necessary to take great care to ensure the highest degree of accuracy.

Shapes

Any shape can be used but is is usual to use symmetrical shapes. These may be triangles, squares, diamonds, hexagons, octagons, lozenges. Some patchwork items are made using only one shape but there are often several different shapes in one piece of work.

The choice of shape is of course entirely personal but those which do not have a sharp angle are easier to deal with. A hexagon is a good shape to use to begin.

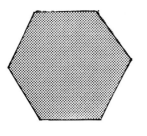

Hexagon

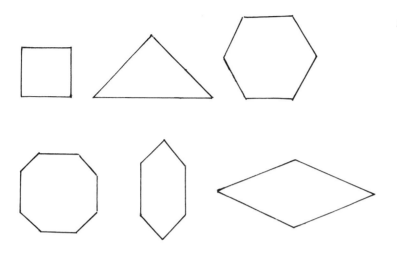

Some popular patchwork shapes

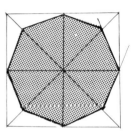

Making templates
A sharp pencil, ruler, set square and a pair of compasses are needed together with some stiff card.

Octagon from a square

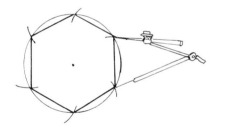

◄ *A hexagon begins with a circle*

Diamonds and triangles can be made from a hexagon

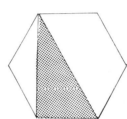

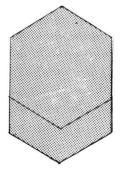

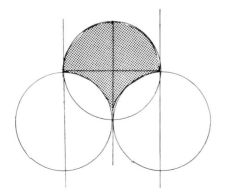

A long hexagon or church window

◄ *A clamshell*

The shapes for this star pattern are built up from two triangles.

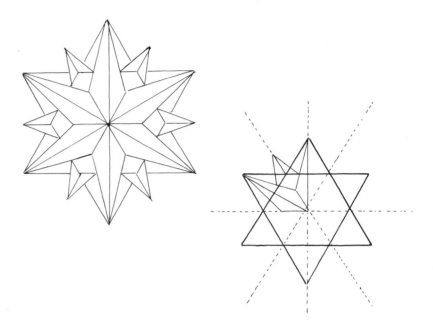

Certain combinations of shapes have become established and been given names so that they can be easily described.

Kaleidoscope

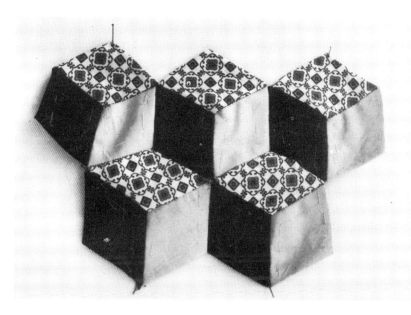

Box pattern using one diamond shaped piece

Making the patches

With a sharp pencil the solid template is drawn round very carefully on to the stiff paper. The stiff paper should then be cut out. Some workers become deft and are able to cut the shapes accurately just by holding the stiff paper and solid template firmly together in one hand. It may be preferred to make all the paper shapes which will be needed to complete the article before going any further.

The paper patches are pinned to the material, making sure that one, and if possible two, straight sides of the paper run along the straight grain of the material. The material should be cut out leaving a half centimetre seam allowance.

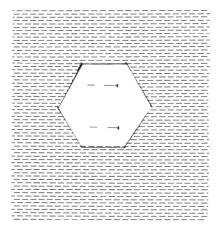

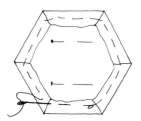

The paper shapes are not taken off the material. The seam allowance is turned over the paper and tacked down all round each patch.

Several patches should be prepared and then they are ready to be joined together.

Joining the patches
The patches should be placed right sides together. Using small stitches one edge of each patch is sewn to one edge of another patch. To begin, the thread should be laid along the top of the edge and sewn over. To finish off four stitches should be worked backwards.

The needle should always be pushed in at right angles to the edge so that the stitches will be neat on the right side.

Patches may be joined in small groups which can then be joined together or in strips or just continuously.

When all the sides of a patch have been joined, the tacking stitches can be taken out and the paper shape comes away quite easily.

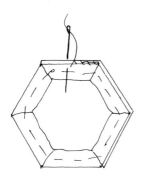

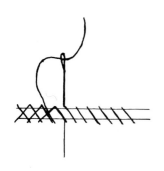

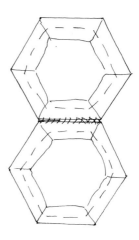

Clamshell patchwork
This is one of the most difficult patchwork shapes to handle satisfactorily. The fabric to be used must be supple and fairly fine as too thick a fabric will not fold over the curve.

These patches are joined in overlapping rows right sides out. The curved top of the first row should be worked against a straight edge. The second row of patches is laid over the lower part of the first, tacked and then sewn round the curved edge with tiny hemming stitches.

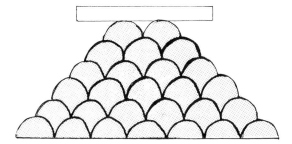

Clamshell patchwork

Suffolk puffs

This variety of patchwork is sometimes known as the Yorkshire Daisy, the Puff Ball or the Yo Yo. A circle is needed for the template and a saucer would be satisfactory. The edge of the circle is turned over and stitched with a gathering thread. The thread is pulled up tight and the puff is flattened.

Suffolk puffs

The circles are joined in four places. This kind of patchwork is generally lined, taking care that the lining fabric is appropriate for the colour and texture of the puffs.

The edge turned in 0.5 cm and gathered

The flattened puff

Log cabin patchwork

This variation on the patchwork idea is unique as the pieces of fabric are stitched to a background fabric as the work progresses.

Log Cabin patchwork relies on light and dark shading of the pieces for its effect.

The centre patch, say 3 cm square is tacked on to a cotton background which needs to be 16.5 cm square with the diagonal lines marked with a tacking stitch. The remaining material which is to be used for the long patches should be cut into strips 3 cm wide and as long as possible.

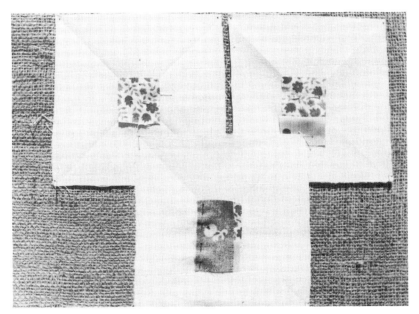

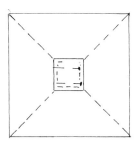

The first patch is tacked in place

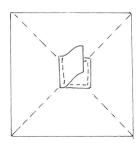

The second patch is attached

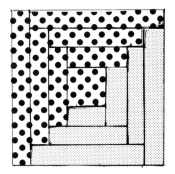

◄ *Log cabin*

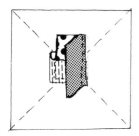

The third patch

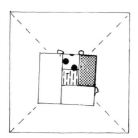

A complete round

The patches are attached by running stitches with 0.5 cm seam allowance.

As each patch or strip is attached it is folded back so that the seam does not show. The next patch is attached like the second one, making sure that it is long enough to cover the end of the previous patch.

Cathedral window patchwork

This term does not describe a particular shape but a method of constructing rather unusual patchwork. For the background patches squares of material are needed about 15 cm square. The edges are folded to form a single hem. The corners are brought to the centre and pinned. The patch should be turned over and again the corners are brought to the centre where they are caught firmly together in opposite pairs.

When several pieces have been prepared they should be over-sewn together in the normal way treating the side with the second folds uppermost as the right side.

The final stage consists of attaching a small patch of contrasting fabric over the joins of the patches. The raw edges of this small patch are covered up by turning back the top-most folds of the background patches. Stab or running stitch is used for this part of the process.

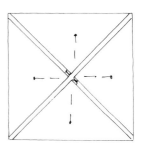

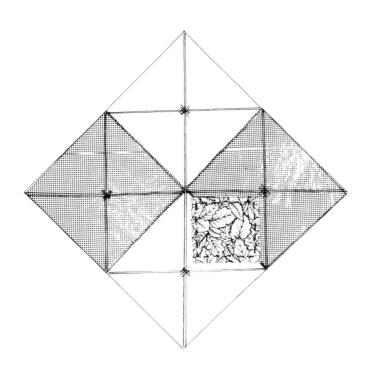

*A small patch is tacked over the
seam where the patches are
joined*

*The folds of the back-
ground patches are sewn over
the raw edges of the small
patch with a running stitch*

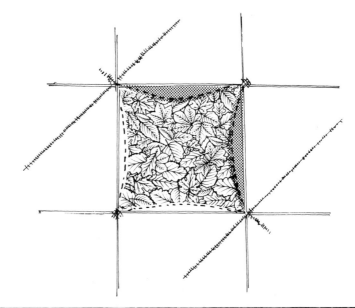

*Cathedral window patchwork
with two sections complete.
The third section is being sewn
with stab stitch and the fourth
section is pinned in place*

Finishing off

Patchwork should be pressed on the wrong side before any papers are taken out. After the first pressing the papers and the tacking stitches should be removed. The work should be tacked round the edge to hold the turnings of the outer patches. The work should be pressed again on the wrong side.

Making up

Unless the finished work is to be made up into a cushion or stuffed toy, some sort of lining is essential. In some cases interlining is used for warmth and sometimes patchwork is quilted. There are many possibilities here but it is mostly a matter of commonsense to find an appropriate material for the lining, making sure that it is attached firmly and neatly.

Leather patchwork

A different approach is needed for patchwork using leather. As leather does not fray, no turnings are needed. Paper patterns are unnecessary too as the shapes can be drawn directly on to the leather which can then be cut out.

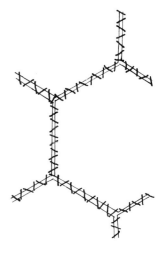

The weight of the leather and the use to which the finished patchwork is to be put decides the technique for joining the patches. They can be placed with the edges butted together and stitched by machine using a close zigzag stitch.

For a stronger finish, a thin strip of leather can be glued at the back of the patches where they are joined. The patches can then be straight machined, zigzag stitched, or joined with an embroidery stitch such as cross stitch.

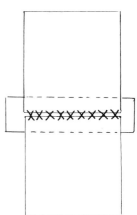

An easy way to join leather pieces is to lay the edge of one patch slightly over the edge of the other and either machine, back stitch or use a small running stitch to hold them together. The clamshell pattern would be very suitable for leather patchwork.

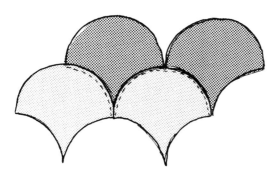

It is very effective to use leather for crazy patchwork where irregular shapes are sewn together at random.

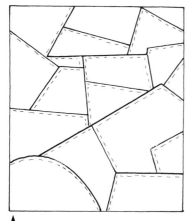

Crazy patchwork

Crazy patchwork using leather pieces

Patchwork for your project

1 Collect scraps and pieces of material for your bit box.
2 Make or buy a collection of geometrical shapes in various sizes.
3 Borrow or buy as many books as possible on the subject.
4 Begin to practise joining a variety of patches together until you have a collection to mount on card for your folder.
5 Experiment with different materials, colours, shapes and combinations of shapes.
6 Start a collection of postcards, slides and pictures showing examples of patchwork. Museums and historic houses will be able to help.
7 Begin a card index system or loose-leaf folder in which to keep notes on the history of patchwork, fabrics for patchwork, traditional patchwork designs, articles I have made in patchwork or any other headings which fit your needs.
8 Plan a finished article or articles which you are going to make to demonstrate your skill in patchwork.

5 Quilting

5 Quilting

Quilting is the process of stitching two layers of fabric together. There may be a layer of wadding or other warm material between the two layers of fabric which will give added warmth or protective qualities to the finished article. Quilting may be purely decorative and have padding or cord in between the two layers of fabric where the design will be made more attractive by a raised effect.

An ancient skill
Quilting is an ancient art. English knights of the Middle Ages wore quilted jackets beneath their armour. In the Tower of London there is exhibited a soldier's jacket from Tudor times of quilted canvas which has pieces of flat metal, diamond shaped, fixed between two layers of linen material. During the seventeenth century quilting became increasingly popular for decorative as well as practical purposes. Examples of quilting can be found on bedcovers, waistcoats, stomachers and hats of this period. About a hundred years ago in the mining districts of County Durham and South Wales a tradition of creating quilted bed covers developed. Their patterns became famous and have been handed down through successive generations. They would have a strong central design.
Round the edges there would be a flowing border pattern.

Twist

Chain

The centre section of a traditional quilt

Wadded or English quilting
Where the quilting is carried out on two layers of material with a layer of wadding or other fabric between these two layers it is generally known as wadded or English quilting.

A quilting design is simple to work out. Provided no area larger than about 6 cm is left without stitches there is no restriction on the pattern which can be used.

Method A
A simple design could be drawn on paper the same size as the finished article will be.

 A tea cosy design

Most template designs begin with a circle

Method B

Cut out some cardboard templates. Arrange and re-arrange these until a satisfactory effect is arrived at. The templates could be geometrical, petal or leaf-shaped or the simple shapes which build up into such elaborate designs used by the quilters of our northern counties and South Wales.

Many of the traditional quilt patterns have names such as twist, rose, star and shell but these names vary from district to district and there is no 'correct' description.

Marking the design

The transfer method traditionally used by quilters is needle-marking. To do this the pattern shapes of the design need to be cut as templates in cardboard or stiff paper. These are then laid onto the top fabric. The template is then outlined with the point of a large thick needle. The needle should be held almost horizontally so that the point scratches the surface of the fabric and does not keep going through it. The design can be drawn in sections while it is being worked or it can be done first by laying the fabric over a fairly soft surface and drawing the design out with the needle.

Dressmakers' carbon paper is used sometimes. The design is traced onto the fabric from the design with the carbon paper placed between. Where there is any chance that the traced line will show when the work is finished then the design must be traced onto the backing fabric and the work carried out from the back. This entirely depends on the stitch which is being used and the fabric. Work a small sample first to see the effect of the carbon paper.

The circle can be folded across its centre into any number of sections

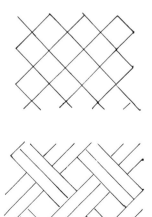

Straight lines are often used for background fillings

Part of a panel with the design drawn on the backing, the layers have been tacked from the front to prevent the machine foot catching the tacking threads

Materials used

Three layers of material are needed for wadded quilting; a backing, a filling such as wadding and a top fabric. Various materials are suitable:

Top fabric　Cotton, linen, satin, silk, velvet.

Padding   Blanket, flannel, domette (a wool and cotton mixture fabric). Wadding which is available by the yard and may be made of terylene.

Backing   This can be the same as the top fabric although a non-slippy material should be used for a bed quilt backing. For economy or comfort a different material may be chosen for the backing but it must be firm, strong and evenly woven. If the material is closely woven, soft and smooth and easy to sew through then it should quilt well.

Thread   The thread must be strong. It depends on the material being quilted, matching silk with silk and cotton with with cotton, giving first consideration to the surface material.

Frames   Quilting can be carried out quite satisfactorily in the hand. A rectangular frame, which consists of two long bars and two flat pieces which fit through slots in the bars and are held in place by pegs fixed in holes, may be used. These are found in various sizes.

When a frame is used the background fabric may be mounted into the frame. The padding is smoothed over this and the surface fabric tacked firmly round the edge.

Alternatively the three layers can be tacked together before they are put into the frame. The bottom layer should be laid flat on the table. The padding is put on top and finally the top layer. The three layers should be tacked together starting from the centre, working horizontally across the work. Several rows of tacking are sometimes needed.

The three layers tacked together horizontally

Stitches used

The most frequently used stitch today is a small even running stitch.

Back stitch was once widely used but is not so popular now.

Chain stitch is used sometimes and also stem stitch.

Where the design is suitable quilting can be done quickly using a sewing machine.

The design begins to appear in relief on the top fabric

Running stitch

Right side

Wrong side

Back stitch

When the stitches are hand-worked each stitch must be made through all three layers of material in two separate movements; one downwards and the other upwards. One hand should be above and the other beneath the work. The needle is stabbed through with the lower hand. The upper hand takes it and returns it directly through the three thicknesses. To maintain tension and keep the work smooth the whole design must be worked gradually forward a little at a time rather than say working the border first. It may be necessary to use more than one needle so that the design can advance evenly.

To begin work make a knot and put the needle in from the underneath. Bring it out on top and pull firmly until the knot slips through the bottom layer and stays in the padding. To finish off make a single back stitch and run the thread in through the padding, cutting the end further along. A small back stitch might be preferred as a beginning stitch.

Stem stitch

Italian or Corded quilting

This form of quilting is used purely for decoration and not for warmth or protection. Two layers of material are needed. The design is worked with two rows of outline stitches and a cord or thick wool is threaded through the narrow channel which is made through the two layers of material. This produces a raised effect.

In Italian quilting the cord which is threaded through the double row of stitching gives a raised effect

Suitable materials
For the surface: Silk, satin, taffeta, velvet, fine wool, linen, cotton.
For the backing: closely woven muslin, cotton
For the insertion: Quilting wool, cord, yarn, knitting wool.
Thread: cotton or silk

A pattern suitable for Italian quilting

Templates are not used for Italian quilting. Floral designs, scrolls and interlaced patterns are suitable.

The design can be traced on to either the surface material or the backing fabric. This depends on whether or not the stitch which is being used will cover the design lines. If a running stitch is being used then it will probably be necessary to draw the design on the backing material. Machining or back-

A sketch of trees to be used for an Italian quilting sampler

stitching might cover the design lines but a small sample needs
to be made first to make sure.

The two layers of material are tacked together and the outline of the design is stitched with small neat running stitches,
back stitches or machining worked in two parallel lines between
3 and 5 mm apart. This is to form channels through which
the padding will be threaded.

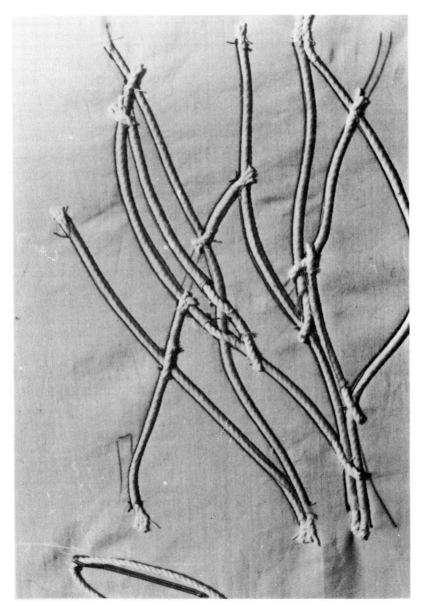

*The ends of the cord are sewn to
the backing*

The insertion is put in from the wrong side. Using a large eyed blunt needle the wool or cord is threaded through the two layers of material, keeping it within the channels made by the running stitches. Where there is a definite angle or curve the needle is brought out through the muslin backing and re-inserted through the same hole leaving a little of the wool or cord to form a loop. The cord should never be pulled tightly. This prevents the padding from pulling or wrinkling.

With the cord inserted between the machined channels the raised effect becomes apparent

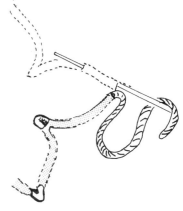

◄ *Outline the design with two rows of small neat stitches*

A loop of cord must be left out of the muslin backing at every corner

A sewing basket lid decorated with Italian quilting

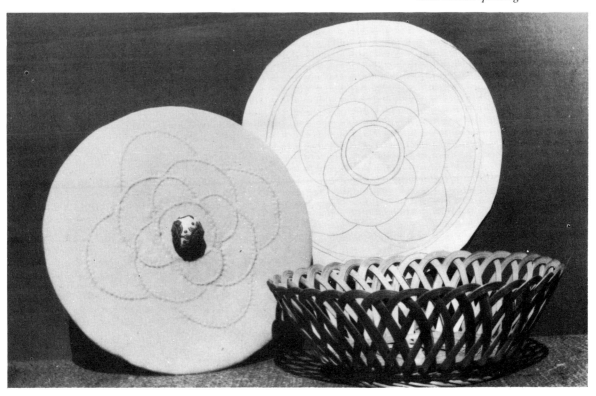

The base of the lid has trapunto quilting which can be used to keep pins and needles

Trapunto quilting
Two layers of fabric are needed for this work. Suitable materials are similar to those which are suggested for Italian quilting. The design areas are outlined with stitching and stuffed afterwards with animal wool, cotton or kapok. Polyester stuffing is light, washable and does not stick together. The designs should not be made up of large plain areas as these are difficult to stuff evenly.

The design should be drawn on to the backing fabric. When this has been outlined, generally with running stitch, through both thicknesses using matching thread, each area is padded separately. A tiny opening should be made in the backing and then the stuffing carefully pushed in using a crochet hook or blunt end of a needle. The hole is then sewn up.

Trapunto quilting is sometimes used together with Italian quilting to create a more varied effect. It is sometimes used too, together with applique embroidery.

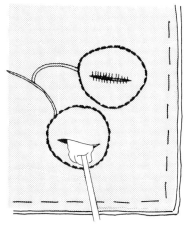

The stuffing is pushed through a small slit which is afterwards sewn up with fishbone stitch

Suggestions for a project on quilting

1 Have a look at as many pieces of quilting as you can through book illustrations, visits to museums or houses. There may be a variety of examples on your own home ranging from quilted anoraks, dressing gowns, tea cosies. Make sketches of the designs and note the materials and paddings which were used.

The basket lining tacked ready for quilting

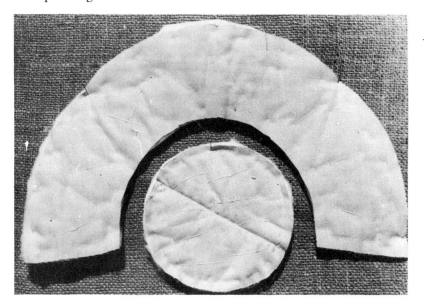

2 Make samples of English or wadded quilting which will show the effect of using different stitches; running stitch, chain stitch, back stitch. Choose two or three different fabrics of contrasting texture such as cotton, silk and velvet and work a similar motif to see the different effects.

3 Make samples which will show how the raised effect of Italian quilting is changed according to the different kinds of wool or yarn which can be threaded through the channels.

4 Try the effect of Italian quilting by choosing a semi-transparent material for the upper surface and threading a contrasting coloured yarn through the lines of the design.

5 Work some trapunto quilting using muslin or firmly woven backings such as cotton sateen to see which is the most satisfactory.

6 The quilting of many articles can be carried out on a sewing machine. Generally this needs careful tacking over the complete area before working as the machine presser foot tends to push the layers out of place. Try a small sample of wadded quilting by machine to overcome this difficulty.

7 Many modern machines are designed for stitching to be done with a double sewing needle. This can be used to do Italian quilting very quickly.

8 The samples should be mounted on card together with samples of the cords or wadding used. Illustrations could be added to show what you might think would be suitable applications for any particular sample you have worked.

9 Choose a method of quilting which you have enjoyed and decide what sort of article you would like to make. Quilting is frequently used for cushions, bags, cot and bed covers, jackets, waistcoats and yokes and hems of dresses. Make sketches and a finished drawing of what you are going to make.

10 Look at fabrics which might be suitable for carying out the quilting design. Small samples of those materials which you consider suitable but you will not have time to work could be mounted on card. You might be pleased to refer back to these later.

11 Decide on the processes which you will use in carrying out the design. Try out the stitches you have chosen on a small sampler and incorporate the padding to make sure that you will be satisfied with the finished effect.

6 Preparing a project

6 Preparing a project

Choosing the subject
It is often difficult to decide what to tackle as a subject for a project. Have a look at projects done by other students. Look at lists of project suggestions. Listen to all the advice you are offered. Consider your own interests and talents. Unless you enjoy working neatly and accurately, for example, do not consider patchwork. Do not be persuaded or rushed when choosing a subject as this can lead to wasted work which is often not enjoyed. Have a look at as many books as possible. Look at finished pieces of work. Sometimes inspiration comes from unexpected places. A piece of braid might start an interest in decoration on clothes, and a wealth of ideas could flow from that. Take care not to choose a topic which is too wide for you to develop fully. If you are going to do embroidery, make sure you realise the scope of the subjects and perhaps choose one or two aspects and explore them thoroughly.

Some suggestions for subjects
The different aspects of embroidery lend themselves to becoming subjects for projects and it is satisfying to become skilful in at least one section of a very wide subject. Some examples are:

> Appliqué
> Assisi
> Beadwork
> Blackwork
> Cross stitch
> Canvas work
> Crewel embroidery
> Gold work
> Patchwork
> Quilting
> Smocking

Knitting, crochet, lacemaking would also provide ample material for a project

There are many aspects of dressmaking which can be studied. The history of costume can be tackled in various ways. You could take a single century and have a look at the clothes worn by all classes of society in Victorian times for example, noting the changes which took place within the period. Such a historical figure of Henry VIII and his six wives could provide the focus for a project on Tudor Costume. A broad look could be taken at the development of clothing from stoneage man up to the present day. One particular article of clothing could be chosen such as headgear, footwear, underwear and the changes which have taken place here could be observed. Many countries have a recognizable national costume and anyone interested in geography might like to study these.

The actual construction of clothes also provides a wide range of subjects for projects:

    Methods of disposing of fullness
    Decorative seams
    Adding decoration to clothes
    The development of the sleeve/collar/bodice
    Methods of making openings

Wardrobe planning for specific activities such as sport, special occasions, a holiday or a wedding would be useful. A layette or clothes for a child say from one to five years could be linked with a study of child development and its needs at a particular age.

Materials used in dressmaking is a complicated study today. An enquiry could be made into man-made fabrics, their origins, manufacture and characteristics. Man-made fabrics could be compared with more traditional fabrics and experiments carried out to measure their advantages as far as heat retention, washing and wearing characteristics are concerned. This sort of topic might appeal to the more scientific minded student.

The equipment needed for needlecrafts is wide-ranging. What equipment is essential? What additional aids are there and how useful are these? Pressing equipment and the sewing machine would provide a great deal of scope for individual study and research.

There are topics for study which might appeal to anyone interested in domestic science or interior design such as soft furnishing, lampshade making, cushions, curtains, wall hangings.

The suggestions so far are rather general and it could be that you have a particular hobby which might be the basis for a project or study. A doll collection might be developed into a topic on the history of dolls. A horse-lover might like to tackle the representation of horses in fabric and thread through applique, cross stitch, toy making. The same could be done with houses. A collection of handbags made with different materials and techniques could be prepared. Jewellery which can be made using needle, fabric and thread is varied and leaves scope for original and imaginative ideas. Soft toy making is satisfying and useful and there are many aspects to this apparently simple subject which can be looked into, such as types of stuffing, wiring, jointing, working with fur.

Perhaps these suggestions are rather overwhelming. It might be a good idea to read them through and then leave the whole subject alone for a week. Often the certainty of what particular subject you might like to study in depth comes to you most surely when you have not been consciously trying to reach a decision.

Where to get information on the subject

The most obvious place to get information on the subject of your choice is, of course, books. Look at as many as possible. Do not rely on just one or even two to get a good grasp of a subject, as you must realise that each book you read on any one subject is only the author's own personal idea of what is important or appealing about a particular subject. Never copy whole pieces from a book. It is not useful for you and the examiner soon spots this.

Museums can be helpful if you write to them and explain what your interests are. The library will give you guidance about museums and historic houses which might be able to help you. From these sources you might be able to buy post-cards, slides and publications. They sometimes provide lists of articles which they have and which you may possibly be able to go and see and then write about them and draw them.

Do not neglect your own local museum or friends who might have pieces of work tucked away which they are often pleased to lend for you to examine, draw or photograph to include in your project.

How to store information as it is acquired

Many people have found it useful to prepare a card index system in a shoe box for example, where items of information can be filed as they are acquired. The titles on the cards would of course entirely depend on the subject and your approach to it. Others prefer a loose-leaf notebook with card to separate different sections. This is purely a matter of personal choice. If this system is kept methodically it will eventually be the guide to the chapter headings of the finished project. For example, if you had tackled toy making you might have received a list of kinds of toy fillings with prices and samples from one or two suppliers. You would then make a card index heading

'Toy fillings; prices and samples'. You might then have read instructions on jointing toys and copied some diagrams from a book. 'Jointing toys' would then be another heading in your index cards. The important thing is to be methodical to avoid a great deal of work at the end of the project sorting out notes and deciding on chapter headings.

Essentials for inclusion in a project

It is most important that the person who is going to read the project can find their way about your information easily. It is essential that the project is divided into sections or chapters and these sections must be headed. The headings should be listed on a contents page, complete with page numbers, at the beginning of the project. A project on doll making might have such sections as:

> Patterns for dolls
> Materials for doll-making
> Tools
> Stitches
> Dolls I have made
> Dolls I have seen

Each project must have a bibliography. This is a list of the books which you have looked at whilst preparing your work. These should be listed in alphabetical order of the author's name. There is a standard method of setting out a bibliography. First you put the author's surname, then initials. Next you write the title of the book, followed by the name of the publisher, place and the year, e.g.:

> Riley, P., *Needlecraft Projects* Batsford London, 1978.

Later on in your studies you might need to refer again to your original sources and you will need this information to give to a librarian or bookseller.

Order of presentation

Many people prefer to include an introduction to give the reader some idea of what to expect in the project. An introduction sometimes gives an interesting insight into how the writer came to tackle the subject. After the introduction many people like to do an elaborate title page but this is not essential. The contents page should follow and then the actual work divided into sections or chapters. Finally you should include the bibliography and a note of the sources you have used for any other information or pictures which have been included. Sometimes an acknowledgment of special help is added but again this is not essential.

How the work should be presented

Mostly the work is presented in loose-leaf folders which are ideally suited for this purpose. If you are not going to use a new folder then it should be given an attractive cover to make it look fresh and appealing. Often the cover is used to show the sort of work you have done. For example a cover may be embroidered or given an appliqué picture to introduce the project.

Where samples of stitches or processes done on fabric are to be included these should be mounted on firm card. Black makes a good background and shows up clearly various stitches and fabrics. Only one edge of the samples should be mounted so that the examiner can see the back of the work if he wishes. The edges of the samples must be neatened. In most cases zigzag machine stitching or cutting with pinking shears is adequate. The neatening must run with the straight grain of the material and the samples centred or placed on the card so that the margins are regular. In every way the samples should show extreme care in presentation and although it does often take up a good deal of time the finished effect makes this worthwhile. Illustrations should be drawn as carefully as possible. Pencil drawings can look casual and are probably best finished off with pen and ink or fine felt tip.

Choose a colour scheme for your project and keep to the same two or three colours for all the illustrations. This can sometimes be extended to the colours of the materials used in the projects and often into the practical work which is made to accompany the written work.

It might seem rather obvious to comment on this but it is so very important that it must be stressed. Be most careful with spelling and keep your handwriting neat and consistent in size and style throughout the study.

Practical work to accompany the project

More stress is now being placed on the practical work which accompanies the project. You must be prepared to present a well-written folder with samples and practical work to illustrate. Here is a chance for personal choice to really go ahead. A project on Victorian costume could be illustrated by sketches of costume, perhaps making a comparison with up-to-date fashion. It might be possible to borrow examples of Victorian costume as there are still many pieces about which could be displayed with the sketches and written work. If there are no facilities for display then the clothes could be drawn and described so you can show what you have seen. A doll could be dressed in Victorian costume or a garment copied full scale.

If toy making was chosen then two or three toys could be made to illustrate the many processes, materials and stuffings which are part of the craft. Obviously there is no point in duplicating work as the examiner wants to see what you are capable of, not the quantity you can turn out.

What makes a good project
You cannot produce a good project unless you make the right choice of subject. Of course, it must be interesting to you but as well as this you must make sure before you start that you will be able to do some reading about your choice of topic. For instance a topic on Chinese Embroidery of the Sung Dynasty might prove extremely difficult to research.

Information which is acquired must be used correctly, backed up where possible by individual research and experiment. There should be a balance of writing, illustration, original ideas and factual information. You really need to get very involved with your project and then you should be able to show true interest and understanding.

Conclusion
Perhaps the most important piece of advice is not to leave everything to the last minute. Get started as soon as you can and set yourself a regular time which you will spend on your project. Go at once to the library and start to gather your information together. It sometimes takes a week or so to get a specific book so you must be prepared for this. Leave yourself plenty of time at the end to spend on presentation.

I hope that you will enjoy preparing your project. It could be the foundation for a lifetime's study, or an heirloom for your grandchildren!

Index